AUBREY BURL

PREHISTORIC ASTRONOMY AND RITUAL

Second edition

SHIRE ARCHAEOLOGY

Cover photograph
Callanish Standing Stones at dawn, Isle of Lewis.
Photograph reproduced by kind permission of Ian Cowe.

British Library Cataloguing in Publication Data:
Burl, Aubrey.
Prehistoric astronomy and ritual. – 2nd ed. – (Shire archaeology; 32)
1. Archaeoastronomy – Great Britain
I. Title
520.9'361
ISBN-10: 0 7478 0614 4

Published in 2010 by
SHIRE PUBLICATIONS LTD
Midland House, West Way, Botley, Oxford OX2 0PH, UK.
(Website: www.shirebooks.co.uk)

Series Editor: James Dyer.

ISBN-13: 978 0 74780 614 1

Number 32 in the Shire Archaeology series.

First published 1983; reprinted 1988, 1991 and 1997.
Second edition, with new text and colour illustrations, 2005; reprinted 2010.

Printed in China through Worldprint Ltd.

Contents

at its highest in the sky, due south at noon.

Mica schist: a slaty rock composed of regular beddings of quartz and mica. These laminations permit the stone to split easily into thin slabs.

Neolithic: New Stone Age. A pre-metal time when tools and weapons were made of stone, flint, bone or wood. From about 4750 (early) to 2500 (late) BC in Britain and Ireland.

Orientation: the direction of an object from a given position. Sometimes used in place of *alignment* but this is careless usage. All objects will have an orientation whether or not they are aligned on anything.

Orrery: a model showing the movements of the planets around the sun.

Outlier: a standing stone outside a prehistoric monument such as a stone circle.

Parallax: the apparent movement of an object when seen from different positions. The effect of parallax can easily be seen by looking at a nearby object with first the left and then the right eye.

Passage tomb: a megalithic tomb with a long passage leading to a chamber near the centre of the covering mound. Found mainly in the west of Britain and Ireland. In Brittany such tombs are known as *dolmens-à-couloir*.

Quadrant: one of four quarters of a circle that has been divided by north-south and east-west lines.

Recumbent stone circles: Scottish Neolithic and Bronze Age circles of standing stones that rise in height towards a southerly large prostrate block. Slightly different types of recumbent stone circle known as 'multiple rings' occur in south-west Ireland.

Refraction: light rays from a celestial object are bent as they pass into and through the atmosphere causing the object to appear higher than it really is. This effect is known as refraction.

Ring cairns: low cairns of the Neolithic and Bronze Ages, usually surrounded by kerbstones, with a central, uncovered space in which cremations are often found.

Row: a line of three or more standing stones.

Shaman: a medicine man or priest-doctor supposedly having power over the spirits of the natural world.

Solstice: *sol* = sun, *stice* = stand: the sun's 'standstill'. The extreme positions of the sun at midsummer and midwinter when its eastern risings and western settings appear to occur at the same places on the horizon for three or four days in succession.

Wedge tomb: an Irish megalithic tomb consisting of an oval or D-shaped cairn with a wedge-shaped gallery that faces between south and west.

Wessex: Wiltshire and surrounding counties on the chalklands of southern England. A densely populated region in prehistoric times.

1
Introduction

There are two questions about prehistoric astronomy in Britain, Ireland and Brittany. The first is whether it ever existed, whether people did align some of their burial places and shrines on the risings and settings of the sun and moon or whether this is just an illusion created by mistaken interpretations of Stonehenge and other monuments.

The second question is more subtle. If prehistoric astronomy did exist, what was it used for? Were there astronomer-priests scientifically studying the heavens or were the alignments for other purposes, for the dead and for the spirits of the Other-World?

It will be a long time before these questions are fully answered but it is already possible to show what people have thought about these problems and how some solutions are appearing. The list of further reading at the end of the book gives a glimpse of the number of books and articles that have been written.

In 1923 Rear-Admiral Boyle Somerville, a pioneer of megalithic astronomy, wrote: 'The occurrence of orientation in prehistoric structures has long been noticed. It has not, however, received from investigators much more than a passing comment.'

This is no longer true. Archaeologists are recognising that orientation is as important as architecture and artefacts to anyone examining the ritual centres of prehistory. This book demonstrates how far we have gone in these studies, largely owing to the stimulus of scholars such as Gerald Hawkins, Alexander Thom and Clive Ruggles.

Because the radiocarbon method is now known to produce prehistoric 'dates' that are too young, these have been converted into real years. Thus a C-14 'date' of 1200 ± 150 bc for the stone circle at Sandy Road, Scone, in Perthshire offers a broad period between 1600 and 1300 BC. Such conversions bring the dates into line with the accurate astronomical chronology of the sun, moon and stars.

Yet even here there must be a warning. The date of about 1500 BC for Sandy Road may not be the time at which the stone circle was erected. The assay came from charcoal lying with a cremation at the centre of the ring, an interment that may not have been made until the site was very old. The archaeological caveat that 'one date is no date' is just one more challenge for the foolhardy prehistorian as he searches for the truth about antiquity, one foot in treacherous ground, worried head in the clouds.

Paradoxically, trustworthy dates could be obtained from the alignments on rapidly moving stars such as α *Aurigae*, Capella, and α *Canis Majoris*, Sirius, but, disappointingly, such helpful celestial targets are almost non-

and slipshod claims for precision encouraged scepticism among archaeologists – including one of the greatest, Gordon Childe. He was as dismissive as Engleheart, claiming: 'It is fantastic to imagine that the ill-clad inhabitants of these boreal isles should shiver night-long in rain and gale, peering through the driving mists to note eclipses and planetary movements in our oft-veiled skies.'

Like Engleheart he was wrong. But he was to have decades of followers serving as an army of resistance among colleagues, their stubborn opposition often coming from an unwillingness or inability to understand the intricate cycles of the moon's movements, a complexity that gave even the astronomer Sir Isaac Newton a headache when studying the lunar subtleties.

Astronomy would not disappear. Assiduous researchers – Boyle Somerville, Sir Norman Lockyer and, more recently, Gerald Hawkins, Alexander Thom and Clive Ruggles – proved that convincing solar and lunar alignments did exist: a roofbox over the entrance to the passage tomb of Newgrange in eastern Ireland that allowed the rays of the midwinter sunrise to illuminate the burial chamber; other solar orientations at Maes Howe, the passage tomb in the Orkneys; at West Kennet on the Marlborough Downs; at Stoney Littleton, south of Bath; lunar alignments among the earthen long barrows on Salisbury Plain near Stonehenge; sightlines in many stone circles and lines of standing stones.

One of the most astonishing sites is the finely restored megalithic tomb of Gavr'inis in the Morbihan of southern Brittany. It contains not one but two alignments, not just to the sun or to the moon but to both. Its long passage, an art gallery of lavishly decorated pillars, faces south-east towards

2. Newgrange passage tomb, County Meath.

3. Maes Howe passage tomb in the Orkneys.

the most southerly moonrise. There is more. From the south side of the end-chamber to the north side of the entrance a second sightline is directed on the midwinter sunrise.

The builders erected an architectural signpost. Where the solar and lunar lines crossed each other half-way down the passage they placed the only stone with no carvings. It is a rough block of white quartz standing in conspicuous isolation, silently emphasising the astronomical intersection in the tomb.

Gavr'inis, 'the island of goats', was never a scientific observatory for astronomer-priests; it was a place of supplication. In it death, superstition, fear and astronomy mingled like shields against the threatening forces of nature. Endangered societies safeguarded themselves through rituals that centred on the sun and moon.

The yearly movements of those heavenly bodies need explanation.

4. The decorated passage in Gavr'inis passage tomb, Gulf of Morbihan, Brittany. The plain quartz pillar is the first stone on the left.

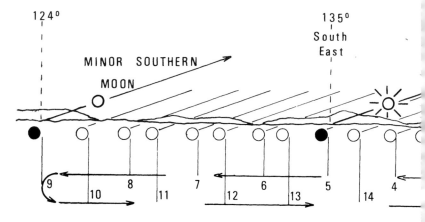

Figure 1. Annual extreme risings of the southern full moon over the 18.61 year lunar cycle. The south-east horizon at latitude 55 degrees north. The extreme rising positions of the sun and moon are shown as solid black rings. Notice how hills affect the places where sunrise and moonrise appear on the skyline.

These azimuths would be different in another latitude. Outside the north-east entrance of Stonehenge, the Heel Stone outlier, with an azimuth of 51°, stands almost in line with the midsummer sunrise. Had Stonehenge been erected in the Orkneys the midsummer sun would have risen at about 38° east of north and the Heel Stone would have stood over 15 metres closer to the north.

The sun is simple; the moon is complex. The place where it rises moves along the horizon just as the sun does but whereas the sun takes a year to complete its NE–SE–NE cycle the moon takes only a month, the time it takes to circle the earth.

Its risings and settings move swiftly from one extreme to the other in a fortnight, waxing and waning from full moon to crescent to invisibility when it is 'new'. Sometimes it rises in daylight so that when darkness comes it can be high in the sky. Another difficulty in observing the moon is that it can be full only when it is opposite the sun, which provides its light. At midwinter, when the sun is at the south, a full moon would be at the north. When the sun, moon and earth are more or less in line it is called the *syzygy*. The moon is new and in darkness when it is between the sun and the earth. It is full and bright when it is on the far side of the earth from the sun.

The rapidity of the moon's movements, its changing shape and its periodic disappearance must have intrigued, perhaps awed, prehistoric people. Because it was a body easily seen at night and capable of being looked at with the naked eye many alignments were directed towards it.

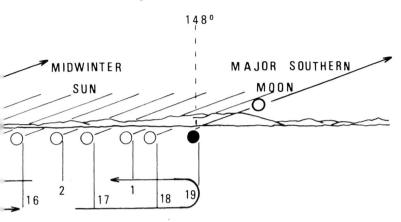

It has, however, a third and considerable handicap.

Its extreme positions both at north and south expand and contract over a period of 18.61 years. At latitude 55° an observer one year would see the midsummer full moon rise at its southernmost extreme around 148°. Unlike the sun's, however, this standstill point was not unalterable. Instead, in succeeding years the moon rose farther and farther southwards from 148° until after nine years it reached as far south as 124°, its minor standstill. In that year the full moon would rise there at midsummer, setting at 236°, and at midwinter it would rise at 56° and set at 304°. Then it would begin its slow return to its major standstill when its midsummer and midwinter arcs were from 148° to 212° and from 32° to 328°.

So involved is this lunar cycle, together with the added confusions of the rapid monthly movement and frequent daylight ascents, that it would have taken years of observations, spanning generations, for prehistoric people to be certain that they had located the standstills accurately. Even professional astronomers have found such lunar variations a challenge. One of the greatest, Sir Isaac Newton, complained that it was only thinking about the movements of the moon that gave him a headache.

Figure 1 shows what our imaginary observer would have seen on the south-eastern horizon at his latitude of 55°. The sun rises at the winter solstice at 135°. The moon at its major standstill rises at 148°. Each succeeding year it will rise farther from the south until it reaches the minor standstill at 124°. Similar diagrams could be drawn for the north-eastern, north-western and south-western skylines.

midget passage tomb. Three rows of stones and an avenue lead up to the ring like the arms of a buckled Celtic cross. It is a unique design and the challenge of its radiating lines has been met earnestly by astronomers.

When this 'Stonehenge of the North' was first described by John Morisone around 1680 he thought the stones were simply men 'converted into stone by ane Inchanter' and set up in a ring 'for devotione'. A few years later Martin Martin also said it was a temple built 'in the time of Heathenisme', but by 1720, convinced that sun-worshipping druids had erected it, John Toland wrote that 'this temple stands astronomically ... dedicated principally to the sun'.

This was the first suggestion that Callanish was more than a rough ring of unworked stones heaved upright by savages for atrocious rites and it was the beginning of a tendency to regard it as a piece of elegant engineering. In 1743 William Stukeley, also certain of the abilities of the druids, optimistically added mathematical exactness to the ring by writing, inexactly, in his *Abury* that 'the circle is 20 cubits in diameter' (10.6 metres, assuming that his 'cubit' was a druidical measure of 52.8 cm).

By 1808 Thomas Headrick, an antiquarian, stated that the circle was laid out to the cardinal points of north, east, south and west to mark 'the rising of the sun, moon and stars, the seasons of the year, and even the hours or divisions of the day'. He had turned Callanish into the megalithic equivalent of an orrery or planetarium.

Daniel Wilson, writing in the mid nineteenth century, called Callanish 'a memorial of primitive astronomical knowledge' but added that it was connected 'with native rites of worship in prehistoric times'. Hardly more than a century ago, therefore, the circle was still thought of mainly as a temple for druidical sacrifice, albeit with some astronomical lines built into it.

This equable mixture of ritual and astronomy might have been acceptable in the religious-cum-scientific atmosphere of Victorian times but by the early twentieth century the astronomy became dominant. Sir Norman Lockyer, director of the Solar Physics Observatory, analysed a plan of Callanish and deduced that the east row pointed to the rising of the Pleiades in 1330 BC and that the avenue to the NNE indicated the rising of the bright star Capella in 1720 BC.

Rear-Admiral Boyle Somerville made his own survey of Callanish in 1909. From it he calculated that the avenue was directed northwards to Capella in 1800 BC, the east row aligned on the Pleiades in 1750 BC, the south row exactly on the meridian, and the west row aligned on the equinoctial sunsets of March and September.

By the 1960s a computer enabled Gerald Hawkins to discover ten good alignments on the sun and moon at their extremes and another on the moon when it was highest at the south. 'The astronomical alignments

6. Callanish from the south row. The west row is on the left of the ring, the east row on the right.

are indisputable', he wrote in *Stonehenge Decoded*, and he pointed out that in that latitude the southern full moon only just rose above the horizon, making its low path across the sky very dramatic.

Callanish was rapidly losing its role as a ritual temple. Increasingly astronomy was replacing ceremony and sacrifice. To Alexander Thom in 1967 the ring was a Type A flattened circle with diameters of 16 by $14^{1}/_{2}$ of his 'megalithic yards' of 0.829 metres. The avenue was 11 megalithic yards (9.1 metres) wide. The southern row was a wonder of exactness, correct to within $0.1°$ of a true north–south line, its precision obtained by the sophisticated bisection of the angle between the east and west elongation of a circumpolar star. Like Somerville, Thom thought the western row was equinoctial and that the avenue was aligned on Capella around 1790 BC; the east row, however, was more probably aimed at the rising of Altair in 1760 BC. He added that 'there is only one obvious explanation of the skew construction at Callanish and that is that the alignments were for astronomical purposes'.

Somerville's plan was slightly inaccurate. A survey of 1974 showed that the azimuth of the east row was $76.5°$ and the declination of $7.8°$ was that of the lovely cluster of the Pleiades rising around 1550 BC. Astronomically it was astonishing because that event seems to have been recorded in the first century BC.

The Greek historian Diodorus of Siculus wrote that in Britain there was 'a spherical temple' at which the moon 'appears to be but a little

8. Ballochroy: a side view to the west, with the Paps of Jura in the background.

neat combination of site selection and astronomical knowledge'.

Yet, although the evidence seems convincing, there are just as good reasons for believing that Ballochroy was not an observatory. The alignment to Cara Island is not precise. Nor could a prehistoric observer have seen the sunset there because a huge cairn 37 metres away from the stones would have blocked his view. It was completely removed years ago when the field walls were built, leaving the cist exposed, but the name of Ballochroy, *baile-cruach* or 'farm by the mound', shows how

9. A view down the row towards the uncovered cist at Ballochroy.

conspicuous this cairn once was. The nearby farm, Cairnbeg, 'the little cairn', still has a mound 3 metres high. This suggests that Ballochroy's cairn was even bigger and when the antiquarian Edward Lhuyd saw it in 1700 he called it 'Karn mor', the great cairn. His sketch shows how it would have obscured any sightline towards Cara.

This does not mean that the people who put up the stones were unaware of the midwinter setting sun. To the contrary, they may have aligned the stones on it as part of the rituals that took place when someone's cremated bones were placed in the cist. But when the funerary ceremonies were over the monstrous cairn was heaped up, as large as the mound at Machrihanish 20 miles (32 km) to the south, 31 metres across, 4.6 metres high, covering a cist like that at Ballochroy. There were standing stones here also.

Nevertheless, even if the south-west alignment at Ballochroy were for the dead this would not explain the very precise and unobscured sightline towards the midsummer sunset at the north-west. This, one would think, had to be intentional. Ironically, it is likely to have been accidental.

Much of the Kintyre peninsula is composed of mica schists that split into thin, broad-faced slabs. These local stones were used at Ballochroy and here geology coincides with astronomy. At that unique latitude the alignments to midwinter and midsummer sunsets form a right angle. The decision to have the broad faces of the stones looking to the south-west meant that each slab had to be set up on a SE–NW axis at 90° to the row. Inevitably each stone was 'aligned' on the midsummer sunset (see figure 1).

If the builders had been interested in this they would have taken great care to line up all the stones on the sunset. As it is, only the central alignment is accurate. The others are not and this suggests that the midsummer orientation at Ballochroy is merely a consequence of the latitude.

Similar coincidences can be found elsewhere. In the Orkneys midsummer sunrise at 39° from north and the minor southern moonrise at 128° happen virtually at right angles to each other. Far to the south at Stonehenge in Wiltshire the alignments to midsummer sunrise at 51° and to the major northern setting of the moon at 321° form an angle of 90° as seen from the centre of the circle. This has prompted claims that the rectangle of the Four Station stones there was designed to record these events.

This does not disprove the theory that Ballochroy was an observatory. It would be unwise for any archaeo-astronomer to ignore possible coincidences, a danger that may be overcome by examining not one but a group of related sites. It is known that there are other three-stone rows like Ballochroy, such as the line of low, bulbous boulders at Torhousekie in Wigtownshire, which is crudely oriented towards midwinter sunset but which does not possess an additional midsummer sightline. The existence of comparable structures with only single alignments must weaken the dual-line interpretation of Ballochroy.

There is another mystery there. There is a third possible alignment along the row towards the north-east, which Gerald Hawkins realised 'points along an elevated horizon towards the extreme northerly position of the moon'. This is true but one wonders if it mattered. The row does point to where the northern moon rises behind a steep hillside; the central stone does line up with midsummer sunset. Even if they knew these things the builders may have been quite uninterested in them, indifferent to anything except the midwinter sunset and the funerary rites around the cist.

In our enthusiasm to discover how prehistoric observatories worked we may be overlooking what prehistoric people thought. It is important to realise that because there is an alignment it does not follow that it was astronomical. There are many instances of monuments with orientations that can never have been related to any celestial event. From the evidence of societies in other parts of the world it is feasible that such sites were set out to face some natural feature or even another monument. Hills or rivers or valleys may have been deemed sacred or connected with an ancestor or some legendary deed. At Callanish it has been argued, entirely sensibly, that the outline of a range of hills to the south, Cailleach na Mointeach – 'the old woman of the moors' – resembles a sleeping woman, but only when seen from the immediate locality of the circle. Such associations with a possible female guardian or deity have been claimed for many other megalithic sites.

Only when an alignment is very precise and defined by man-made structures or when it is consistently repeated in a group of similar sites should it be accepted as astronomical. Archaeo-astronomy demands discipline and unless an entire group of similar monuments, such as the recumbent stone circles of north-eastern Scotland, contain indisputably similar celestial sightlines there can be no assurance that these sightlines were intended by the builders. One is still left with the seminal question 'Why?'

It is dangerously easy to impose our own ideas on the prehistoric sites that we study and to distort them into our image. The beliefs of earlier workers reflected the attitudes and prejudices of their times. In our own scientific age our interpretations tend to be scientific and we are inclined to attribute significance to every alignment that we discover. All researchers are affected by the opinions of the age in which they live.

5
The primitive phase:
burial places, 4000–3000 BC

The earliest investigators of prehistoric astronomy paid most attention to stone circles. More recent workers have included rows of stones in their researches. Perhaps because of this concentration on settings of standing stones it is still not generally realised that many Neolithic tombs, some more than a thousand years older than the first stone circles, also were planned to face the sun or moon.

For a long time archaeologists have known that the axis of a normal long barrow in Britain, so arranged that the mound's wider, higher end covered the burials, nearly always pointed somewhere between NNE and SSE. This is true also of megalithic tombs with stone-lined chambers. The earliest were probably quite small, simple family vaults, but whether the chamber stood at the end of a long cairn, such as Lochhill in Dumfries-shire, erected around 3900 BC, or at the centre of a round passage tomb, like those built some time later at Knowth in County Meath, there was an accepted direction for the entrance to face.

Every region had its own tradition (see figure 3).

10. Cairnholy chambered tomb, Kirkcudbrightshire.

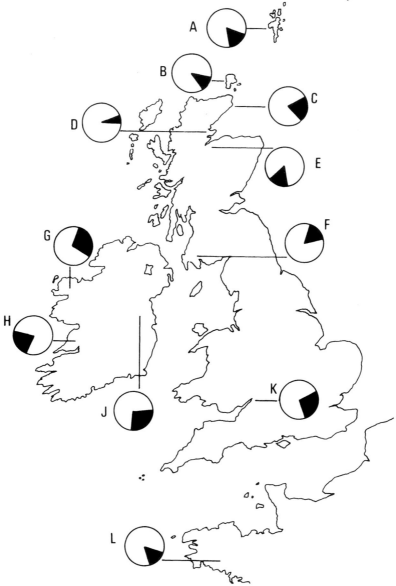

Figure 3. The azimuths of some groups of chambered tombs. (A) Shetland heel-shaped cairns; (B) Orkney stalled cairns; (C) Camster tombs, Caithness; (D) Camster tombs, Ross and Cromarty; (E) Clava Cairns; (F) Clyde long mounds; (G) court cairns, County Mayo; (H) wedge tombs; (J) Boyne passage tombs; (K) Cotswold-Severn long mounds; (L) passage tombs, Brittany.

Almost all these early tombs looked eastwards but whereas the long cairns in the Cotswolds had entrances lying between north-east and south-east those of south-western Scotland, very similar in their architecture to the Wessex barrows, had a much narrower range between NNE and ENE. In Brittany the majority of the entrances clustered around the south-east.

Common sense suggests that these restricted arcs resulted from the tomb-builders aligning their entrances on some astronomical event. Somerville believed that the Hebridean passage tomb of Barpa Langass was aligned on the midwinter sunset. West Kennet in Wiltshire looks towards the equinoctial sunrise. Round Camster in Caithness with its long, east-facing passage may also have been oriented on the equinoctial sun rising over the nearby Hill of Yarrows.

Other societies are known to have linked death with the sun and moon. Neolithic people may have thought these were the homes of ancestors or that their rays would reanimate the souls of the dead. The American painter George Catlin described how Mandan Indians in Dakota would expose a corpse on a high scaffold 'with its feet carefully presented to the rising sun'. Navajo Indians believed that death was a companion of the sun, and in the Pacific the Caroline Islanders said their ancestors died again when the moon waned but revived on its re-emergence as a crescent in the sky.

Beliefs such as these may have led to the earliest known alignments in Britain and Ireland, rough orientations whose accuracy was affected by many other considerations. Some regions may have been content to set a tomb in line with sunrise at any time of the year; others may have believed that only midwinter or midsummer orientations were effective. It is, in any case, unlikely that many of these sightlines were precise. The lie of the land, the quality of the building stone, the skill of the builders, the need to make the tomb conspicuous, all may have influenced the direction of the passage. Moreover, because this passage had to be wide enough to admit a person dragging a corpse or clutching a bundle of skeletal bones the arc of vision from the chamber could be very broad. Such coarse orientations may have satisfied the spiritual needs of a Neolithic family but they do not delight the mind of an archaeo-astronomer looking for indisputable alignments.

To his further discomfiture some tombs may have had no astronomical significance at all. Several cairns of the Carrowmore cemetery in County Sligo were laid out to look not towards the northern moonset but the gigantic mound of Maeve's Cairn on Knocknarea mountain several kilometres to the north-west, perhaps even to the mountain itself. The west-facing passage tomb of Wideford Hill on Orkney is less likely to have been aligned on the equinoctial sunset than upon the probably earlier tomb of Cuween at the other side of a wide fertile plain. One can detect such exceptions because they are exactly that, exceptions to the rule that can be recognised only when whole groups of similar sites are studied.

As well as the alignments themselves there are other clues to the astronomical interests of Neolithic people. Carvings, apparently of suns, in some Irish passage tombs support the idea of a prehistoric association between the dead and the sky, and Martin Brennan believed he had identified a lunar calendar engraved on one of the kerbstones at Knowth in the Boyne valley.

Legends also may help in our search because they too hint at solar or lunar rituals. In Somerset the capstone of the Waterstone long mound is supposed to dance on midsummer's day whenever the moon is full. The massive megalithic *dolmen à couloir* of La-Roche-aux-Fées in Brittany reputedly stands in line with the southern moonrise. The lack of finds in this so-called tomb and the tradition of courting couples counting the stones on the night of the new moon implies that this imposing monument may have been a shrine rather than a grave, a place where Neolithic families held their ceremonies when the moon was bright.

As the centuries of the New Stone Age passed, the tombs gradually lost their role as simple family burial places and became ossuaries in which ancestral bones and skulls were used by the living in rites of fertility and magic. Towards the end of the fourth millennium newly built mounds

11. La-Roche-aux-Fées *dolmen à couloir*, Essé, Ille-et-Vilaine, Brittany.

12. Newgrange passage tomb. The 'letterbox' entrance is above the spiral-decorated slab.

such as Newgrange in County Meath, dated to about 3200 BC, were really grandiose temples, huge structures for the use of large assemblies. In them the alignments were more nicely defined.

Above the lintelled entrance of Newgrange is a narrow, stone-slabbed aperture like a giant letterbox. Such a superfluous feature seemed inexplicable. Legend, however, had it that sunlight somehow penetrated the blocked-up passage and illuminated a triple spiral carved in the dark chamber at the heart of the cairn.

Experiments showed that for a few days around the winter solstice the rising sun shone through the gap of the 'roofbox', its rays reaching down the passage to the three end-chambers in which the bones of the dead had rested. So well planned was this alignment and so ideal was the roofbox that this almost certainly was its intended purpose but had the alignment been for a living observer the aperture would have been unnecessary because the passage would not have been blocked.

It should be noticed, though, that the roofbox was usually closed with two quartz stones that were pushed aside at midwinter. Somebody outside the cairn had to know when this time came and, in that sense, he or she was an astronomical observer.

Since the recognition of this roofbox at Newgrange similar 'windows' have been suspected at the passage tomb of Bryn Celli Ddu on Anglesey and at two small chambered tombs alongside Newgrange. When they

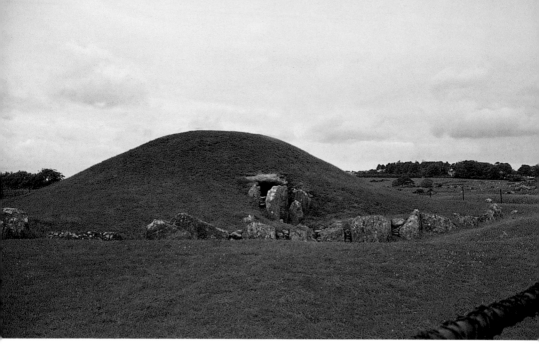

13. Bryn Celli Ddu chambered tomb, Anglesey.

were finally closed, sealing the burnt bones of the dead inside them, these south-facing mounds may have had gaps left above the rubble that blocked their entrances so that the light of the low midwinter sun could shine down their passages at noon. It is this conjunction of the sky and the dead that is the theme of archaeo-astronomy in Britain and Ireland.

At Maes Howe, the superbly designed passage tomb on Orkney built around 2700 BC, a similar slit above the blocking slab may have been intended to allow the glow of midwinter sunset to reach into the central chamber. Maes Howe, erected very late in the megalithic tomb tradition, had an entrance facing south-west. Often in that final phase entrances opened westwards, quite different from the easterly directions of most Neolithic burial places, as though the settings of the sun or moon were becoming more important than their risings. Slieve Gullion, a passage tomb built around 2500 BC on a stupendous mountain in County Armagh, faced south-west, and the scores of wedge tombs in western Ireland, considered to be some of the last of the megalithic tombs, had entrances consistently aligned between WNW and SSW.

This re-orientation, which anticipated the sunset ceremonies of the Iron Age Celts by some 2500 years, is very obvious in the stone-circle-surrounded Clava Cairns of Inverness-shire. Over thirty of these south-west-oriented cairns are known, the first being no earlier than about 2500 BC and the last as late as 1200 BC. Some of them at the head of the

14. Maes Howe passage tomb, Orkney.

15. Balnuaran of Clava passage tomb cemetery, Inverness-shire.

These stone circles are probably as much as five hundred years older than the Inverness-shire sites. Later still are the associated recumbent stone circles of southern Ireland, also with azimuths in the south-west quadrant. If the archaeological links between the three groups are valid, then these cairns and rings provide an astonishing example of continuity from about 3000 BC in Aberdeenshire to as late as 1000 BC in Cork and

17. Balnuaran of Clava, north-east passage tomb. The ranging-pole at the end of the passage shows how the roofing slabs would have restricted the view to the skyline like a 'letterbox'.

Kerry – two thousand years of an unbroken astronomical tradition.

Alexander Thom, and Somerville before him, noticed that the two passage tombs at Balnuaran of Clava near Inverness faced the midwinter sunset. Since then it has been found that other Clava tombs were planned to look towards the southern moon. A provisional calculation of the declinations of the passage-tomb entrances shows a close correspondence with the solar and lunar extremes.

Major southern moonrise (declination -29.1°). Avielochan, -28.8°; Druidtemple, -29.7°; Upper Lagmore, -28.4°.

Major southern moonset (declination -29.1°). Carn Urnan, -29.7°; Croftcroy, -29.1°; Kinchyle of Dores, -29.9°.

Midwinter sunset (declination -24.0°). Balnuaran of Clava, north-east, -24.0°; Balnuaran of Clava, south-west, -24.0°.

Minor southern moonset (declination -18.9°). Carn Daley, -19.0°; Corrimony, -18.9°; Dalcross, -18.9°.

Although these late megalithic 'tombs' contain alignments that were neater and more accurate than those of the early Neolithic mounds there are reasons for doubting that they were observatories for astronomer-priests. First, the sightlines are very broad: no passage is less than 45.7 cm across or longer than 9 metres, so that the narrowest arc of vision from the chamber is 3° wide. Second, the lowness of the passage roof in most of the cairns prevented an observer from seeing the skyline. Presumably, once the solar or lunar alignment had been defined the side-slabs of the passage were erected along the axis, the corbelled chamber was built, capstones were lifted into place and the cairn was piled up over the whole structure. Even if the entrance had been left unblocked the rays of the sun or moon could have reached no more than a metre or so down the passage.

If the sightlines were for the dead this would have been enough. As at Newgrange, the alignments were symbolic and they would continue to be so, even in the vast open-air monuments of the developed phase.

6
The developed phase:
stone circles, 3000–2000 BC

As society grew more complex and as trading contacts expanded it was no longer possible for families to remain self-sufficient, almost isolated from the others, each content with its own place of worship. Communities intermingled and new, larger 'temples' such as Newgrange, later partly encircled by an unfinished ring of stones, replaced the old shrines. During the last centuries of the fourth millennium, in the late Neolithic period, even more spacious, uncovered enclosures were put up for the crowds of people gathering on the great occasions of the year.

Laborious undertakings such as the construction of Silbury Hill or the quarrying of thousands of tons of chalk from Avebury's ditches reveal how well organised societies now were, with powerful leaders to plan and direct the communal projects. It is probable that as society became more stratified, perhaps with priests or shamans as well as chiefs and craftsmen, so the rituals of summer and winter became more formalised. Performed in the circular henges with their earthen banks or in the novel stone circles of the highlands, these ceremonies necessitated the laying out of accurate alignments in the rings, possibly to mark the times of important gatherings.

As in earlier centuries, not every orientation was astronomical. The north–south entrances of henges in Cornwall faced directions where the sun or moon could never have risen or set. Some small henges at Milfield in Northumberland had entrances so arranged that they offered differing views of the horizon. A few miles to their south at Yeavering the opposing entrances of a henge were aligned WNW–ESE towards a 1.8 metre high outlying stone and, beyond it, to the conspicuous hill of Ross Castles 10 miles (16 km) away.

As long ago as 1892 A. L. Lewis said he knew of at least one hundred examples of stone circles that were aligned on outlying stones and prominent hills, and in 1926 Lily Chitty noticed that three gaps in the Shropshire ring of Black Marsh were in line with hills there. The gap at the SSW was particularly noticeable: 'By placing walking-sticks against [stones] 19 and 20 [Corndon] mountain was exactly framed between them.'

This is in keeping with the belief that natural features could also be the focus of alignments. Yet from the centre stone at Black Marsh the two sides of the entrance have azimuths of 195° and 216°. The declination at the midpoint is -29.8°, very close to an alignment on the major southern

18. Black Marsh stone circle, Shropshire.

setting of the moon. This suggests that both the hill and the moon have been targets here – a duality of alignment not unknown in other sites.

At the very beginning of this developed phase people on Salisbury Plain, after years of observations, had the skill to set out two competent sightlines, one to the midsummer sunrise, the other to the major rising of the northern moon. Even today, when the chalk bank is grass-covered and worn down and when several of the outlying stones are missing, this first phase of Stonehenge is still an impressive reminder of the abilities of those early observers.

Sceptics have claimed that the misty weather conditions of Britain and Ireland were such that no refined observations would have been practicable and that, in any case, very few sightlines would have been possible in the thickly forested landscapes of prehistory. They seem to be mistaken. Evidence from the almost indestructible husks of pollen and, somewhat unexpectedly, from the shells of light- and warmth-loving snails shows that during this period the climate was milder and drier than it is in modern times, and less cloudy, the cold and pellucid winter skies providing excellent conditions for astronomical observations. It also shows that great tracts of woodland had been cut down by Neolithic settlers and that many early stone circles and henges were put up on abandoned farming land in an open, treeless landscape.

Not all sightlines were solar or lunar. Cardinal alignments have been noticed at Stonehenge, at Brodgar and Stenness in the Orkneys, Callanish with its straight south-facing short row of stones, the Druids' Temple by Morecambe Bay, Mayburgh near Penrith and in other stone circles and henges, and it seems likely that most of them were set out in quadrants whose primary axis was either to the north–south or to the east–west equinoctial directions. This is true of the fifty-six Aubrey Holes at Stonehenge.

The reasons for the alignments remain contentious. What is even stranger is that the rings frequently had extra sightlines built into them. These can be recognised by the choice of a markedly taller stone or by an entrance or an outlier to act as a foresight. It is these markers that we should study today. The stones should be their own record. It is undiscriminating to accept one convenient notch out of innumerable skyline features unless there is something in the circle that indicates it.

Proof of an alignment demands the existence not only of a target such as the sun or moon but also of a backsight, where the observer stood, and a foresight, to which he looked. In megalithic tombs these might be the chamber and the entrance respectively. In the rings and henges one must assume that the backsight was on the axis and that the foresight was one of the artificial features mentioned earlier.

If such backsights and foresights define an astronomical event one can have some confidence in its significance, especially if it is an event repeated in several comparable sites.

This is certainly true of the stone circles of Cumbria, where, in addition to the cardinal lines, there are other alignments. They seem to be calendrical. At the immense ring of Long Meg and Her Daughters there is a line through the entrance to a tapering outlier and to midwinter sunset. At Castlerigg the backsight of the tallest stone is set axially towards the north-west and the azimuth of 307° produces a declination of +24.3° for midsummer sunset. In the other direction, the line, with a declination of -16.0°, points to Candlemas sunrise on 1st February. The south-east entrance of Swinside near the Cumbrian coast is aligned on the same February sunrise and so is the ruined entrance of the Girdle Stanes in Dumfries-shire. In Perthshire Croft Moraig's entrance looks to the equinoctial sunrise.

A February alignment is not as improbable as one might think. Alexander Thom suggested that the prehistoric year was divided into sixteen equal periods. This deduction may be an over-refinement of a simpler calendar. The eight declinations of every alternate one of Thom's 'months' correspond closely to those of Iron Age feast days three thousand

19. Long Meg outlier and stone circle, Cumbria.

years later. Later still, Christianity adopted and adapted these when the Church struggled to overcome heathen customs. It is ironical that celebrants of All Souls' Day should unknowingly be perpetuating a festival of the dead, Samain, that began five thousand years ago in a pagan stone circle.

20. Swinside stone circle, Cumbria. The two entrance stones are on the far left-hand side of the ring.

23. Druid's Circle, Conwy. Cremations of children were found at the centre.

24. Boscawen-Un stone circle, Land's End, Cornwall. The white quartz stone is on the far side, to the right of the central pillar.

25. Beltany Tops stone circle, County Donegal.

Beltany Tops, a circle in County Donegal associated with the May assembly of Beltane, also has a Samain alignment. From the backsight of a stone covered in cupmarks an axial sightline points to the foresight of the ring's tallest stone at the WSW in line with the sunsets of both Samain in November and Imbolc in February. With more research others of these 'Celtic' calendrical orientations might be detected in henges and stone circles, showing how Neolithic and Bronze Age people held rituals at times of the year more often thought to be associated with Iron Age customs. If, as some claim, the druids originated in the Bronze Age or even earlier there is no reason why the festivals linked with them should not be just as old.

At Stonehenge, the monument most popularly inhabited by druids, Hawkins has suggested that more sightlines were added when the thick circle of sarsen stones was erected. Built around 2500 BC, this heavy ring enclosed a horseshoe-shaped setting of five separate stone archways, each made of two enormous standing stones with a lintel across them. This horseshoe of trilithons ('three-stones') is claimed to possess a complete set of sightlines to midwinter and midsummer sunrises and sunsets and to the southern moonrises and northern moonsets. They are very coarse, some of them several degrees wide, and they remain controversial and unconvincing.

This is not true of all sightlines. In some circles alignments were defined by grading the heights of the stones, as the builders of the Clava Cairns

26. Stonehenge, Salisbury Plain, Wiltshire.

did. Several rings in southern Britain are graded but it is a feature best seen in the recumbent stone circles of north-east Scotland. The cremated bone, quartz, cupmarks and inner ring cairns of these sites anticipated the Clava tradition by as much as five hundred years.

The recumbent stone, a huge block lying between the two tallest stones of the ring, is not to be seen in any Clava Cairn. Yet the southerly azimuths of these great stones, between 155° and 235°, occupying an arc almost identical to the Clava passage-tomb entrances, reveal how long a tradition could endure.

The recumbents, it seems, were aligned on the southern moon. Some rings face the extreme rising of the moon in the south, more face its setting and still others look where the moon would have been high in the southern sky. The normal situation for a recumbent stone circle was on a hillside. From here the moon on the far-off horizon would be neatly framed as it passed between the horn-like stones that flanked the recumbent. It was an accurate but broad alignment. The diameter of an average circle here is about 20 metres, so that with a recumbent stone 3.7 metres long an observer would have had an arc of vision over 10° wide. It would take the moon about an hour to pass across such an arc and this may have been what the users of the ring wanted in their ceremonies. Had they been making scientific observations, however, they would have created a sharper sightline.

Scottish recumbent stone circles continued to be built until a time that overlapped the construction of the first Clava Cairns. It is a period that emphasises how long-lived the tradition was along the coasts of the Moray Firth and in north-east Scotland, a longevity probably caused by the isolation of the followers of that cult.

Their beliefs were not those of the south. The recumbent stone circles, just as closely grouped together as the Clava Cairns, were family monuments, unlike the wide and open communal enclosures elsewhere in Britain in this developed phase. In the recumbent stone circles the lunar alignments brought the moon into association with the dead and the 'sightlines' had a purpose different from the calendrical lines of Cumbria. But in all the regions the circles were well built and the alignments were carefully laid out. It was a fastidiousness that did not endure. As the megalithic tradition slowly waned the astronomy also suffered decline.

7
The local phase:
standing stones, 2000–1250 BC

With the fertile lowlands becoming over-populated, the ending of the early Bronze Age brought widespread settlement in areas that had been almost uninhabited throughout the Neolithic Age. For a few centuries the climate permitted the cultivation of thinner upland soils, and during the early years of the second millennium BC regions such as Dartmoor, the Yorkshire Moors, the Cheviots and the Boggeragh mountains of southern Ireland were farmed by energetic and resourceful families. It was they who erected many of the bleak rings and rows of stones that still stand on today's deserted moors.

In a landscape of long steep hillsides, the valleys between them divided by leaping streams and rivers, the farmsteads of many settlers must have been solitary places. There were few large communities and in the hill country the new ritual centres were small. There was no need of large enclosures, nor did the few men and women have the resources to build them. Instead, they put up inexact and scaled-down versions of the great

27. Midmar Kirk recumbent stone circle, Aberdeenshire. Professor Clive Ruggles is surveying the azimuth. The ring was aligned on the minor southern moonset.

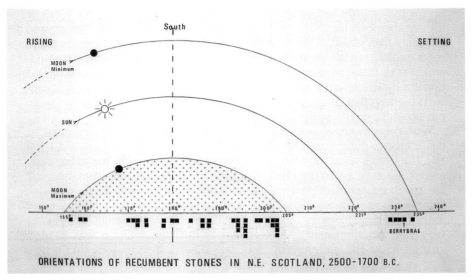

ORIENTATIONS OF RECUMBENT STONES IN N.E. SCOTLAND, 2500-1700 B.C.

28. Diagram of recumbent stone circle azimuths. Each black square represents the declination of one of the forty circles surveyed.

circles and henges, the constricted four-poster rectangles of Perthshire, the cairn circles of Dartmoor, the mixture of henge and megalithic ring to be seen in the unspectacular embanked stone circles of the Peak District.

They were for few people. Deep into Dartmoor, rings such as Down Tor were a fifth the size of Scorhill and other early circles at the edge of the moor. A Scottish four-poster with its central burial pit was no bigger than a modern sitting-room.

There are so many late rings in Britain and Ireland that it

29. Down Tor stone row and circle, Dartmoor.

34. Beaghmore rows and stone circles, County Tyrone.

vary from +22.4° to +26.6° instead of focusing on +23.9°, and for the moon, +26.1° to +31.4° instead of +29.1°. The results were so crude that Archie Thom wondered whether the erectors were mere beginners learning about the moon's movements. In so late a period they were probably peasant farmers struggling with something beyond their ability.

Constantly in these late sites human bone is found. There were cairns between the circles at Beaghmore. In the Peak District, at Barbrook II, built around 1850 BC, John Barnatt thought that Candlemas and Lammas sun-lines and southern moon-lines were built into the axial settings of the ring and he produced a good plan to demonstrate this. The builders may have intended the astronomy but they certainly intended the cist with its cupmarked slab, the pyre, and the cremation under the cairn, which they put up inside the embanked circle. On Salisbury Plain the grave of the little child interred at Woodhenge faced the midsummer sunrise, dug there by people whose beliefs were not the same as ours because their way of life was not the same.

Death was never far from their imagination and the sun and moon were never far from their vision of death. Even in their graves there were orientations. Frequently in the highlands a body or its cremated remains were placed in a slab-lined cist and these cists followed the same tradition of preferred alignments as the megalithic tombs before them. On Dartmoor the cists, over eighty of them, had a predominantly NW–SE disposition. In northern Britain cists with burials accompanied by thick-lugged food vessels were often built with their long sides set north–south.

Even corpses laid in ordinary graves were arranged according to the custom of the region. In Yorkshire burials with fine beaker pots had men with their heads to the east, women with their heads to the west, both facing south. More commonly, both on the continental mainland and in Britain the makers of such pottery preferred to put the bodies in graves that were dug north–south, men's heads to the north, women's to the south, both looking to the east.

A young man buried in a wooden coffin at the centre of a ditched circle near Stanton Harcourt in Oxfordshire, a quiver of arrows at his hip, a beaker by his head, lay crouched with hands on his shoulders, head at the north, looking eastwards through the timber side of his coffin, through the gravel of the grave pit, towards the sunrise. This was never an alignment for the living but it does show how the living followed the solar and lunar traditions when rites were performed for the dead.

These were the realities of astronomical practice. They reveal the intimate, mystical transpositions of sun, moon, life and death in the minds of the same people whose rows and rings of stones frustrate our

35. Roundway Down beaker burial, Devizes, Wiltshire. As was customary, the man was buried with his head to the north, facing eastwards.

understanding. A pair of stones at Orwell in Perthshire had human bone in one of the stone-holes, put there before the stone was raised. At Ballochroy the cist was aligned, like the row there, NE–SW towards the midwinter sunset and it is facts such as these that tell us most clearly that the orientations were symbolic rather than scientific, for obsequies rather than observations.

This belief is confirmed by recumbent stone circles in Scotland and Ireland and by associated monuments. Stones deliberately laid flat, as the recumbents were, seem consistently astronomical. The spiral-carved entrance stone at Newgrange lay across the line of the midwinter sunrise. Martin Brennan believed that a similar stone at Knowth passage tomb was oriented on the equinoctial sunrise. The Scottish recumbent stone circles and their Clava Cairn successors were aligned on important solar and lunar positions.

This is true of related sites also. Croft Moraig in Perthshire, a circle whose stones are graded in height like those of Aberdeenshire, has an eastern entrance. Much less conspicuous is the overgrown stone lying prostrate on the south-west perimeter, its surface pitted with cupmarks (see figure 5).

The cairn at Kintraw in Argyll has the same orientation. This site with its cisted cremation has, like Ballochroy, been acclaimed as a precise solar observatory because a standing stone near it is almost in line with the midwinter sunset. The sunset cannot actually be seen from the cairn,

36. Croft Moraig, Perthshire: cupmarked recumbent stone.

which, in any case, is not in the right place, but the discovery of a possible viewing platform cut into the suicidally precipitous hillside above the cairn has excited some, if not all, archaeo-astronomers.

Kintraw, however, has the disregarded but notable feature of an 'entrance' at its SSW with a long, supine stone in front of it. The entrance, consisting of two standing stones flanking an upright slab, resembled the blocking stone to a passage. Kintraw, however, has no passage, only

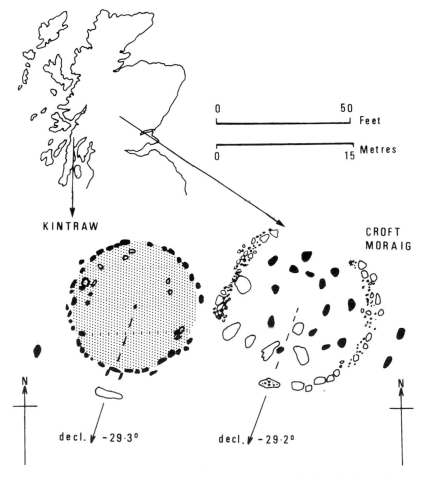

Figure 5. Plans of Croft Moraig, Perthshire, and Kintraw, Argyll, showing the supine stones at their SSW. From the centre of the ring the stone has an azimuth of 200° and a declination of -29.2°, that of the major southern moonset.

showing that the stones were put up around 1200 BC, almost two thousand years after the earliest of the recumbent stone circles of Aberdeenshire.

It is the astronomy that confirms the Clava–Aberdeen–Munster connection. The azimuths in south-west Ireland of 170° to 294° cover the same arc as those of the Scottish chambered tombs and stone circles with the addition of an extension to the WNW. Nineteen of the thirty-two known declinations, those with azimuths between 171° and 235°, are lunar although the short diameters cause wide arcs of vision. The five-stone ring of Rylane, only 3.7 metres across but with a recumbent stone nearly 2.1 metres long, offers an arc from 200° to 230° and although the central declination of -30° is in line with the major setting of the southern moon the lunar alignment is more like a panoramic window than an astronomical peep-hole.

The Irish rings here that do not conform to the lunar pattern are good examples of an intermixing of traditions and act as warnings against facile interpretations. These untypical circles, such as Carrigagulla and Derreenataggart, lie inland where chambered cairns known as wedge tombs had been built by settlers long before the arrival of the stone-circle people. The entrances to these unusual tombs faced between SSW and WNW and it is likely that the incoming circle-builders, mingling with the natives, accepted the older tradition, aligning their own rings not on the moon but on the sunsets of February and November.

Yet, whether the moon or the sun, the astronomy was fused with death. Burnt human bone lay in the wedge tombs, and at the centre of the Cashelkeelty ring was a slab-covered pit in which lay the cremated remains of a young adult. From the vague beginnings in the Neolithic long graves down to these last little stones three thousand years later the associations were the same.

Even with the abandonment of the uplands as the climate worsened, and when the megalithic tradition had faded, some of the customs endured. The occasions of the Celtic festivals demanded the keeping of a calendar. And, in the Iron Age, temples and shrines at Heathrow, Brigstock, Winchester and Danebury faced eastwards. At South Cadbury the porched shrine also faced east and outside its veranda pits with offerings of sacrificed animals lay in line with the equinoctial sunrise. Thousands of years earlier people had buried an ox outside the east-facing entrance of the passage tomb of Bryn Celli Ddu on Anglesey, a tomb that may have had a solar roofbox.

Modern visitors to these ancient places often sense the mysteries contained within the stones but it is our ignorance, not the forgotten powers of a psychic world, that causes our feeling of loss. From the first Neolithic tomb to the last Iron Age temple the stones were not mysteries to the people who raised them.

8
Balquhain: 'the stone that puts the stars to flight'

Like other prehistoric ritual monuments, stone circles exasperate. In 1705, on his travels around south-west England, Daniel Defoe saw Boscawen-Un near Land's End and despaired. There was no carving on the stones, no tradition attached to the ring. 'All that can be said of them, is, that *here they are!*' A hundred years later Byron was equally frustrated at Stonehenge. 'But what the Devil is it?', he cried. Matters did not improve.

'Rude stone monuments' is what Fergusson called the megaliths in 1872. Forty years later Peet was just as dismissive with his description 'Rough'. Both were correct, but they saw only the skin. Despite the rude, rough, rugged, raw appearance, the monuments are also refined and reticent. Their stones are unshaped but skilfully erected and from them come murmurs of ancient beliefs that we are now beginning to hear and maybe understand.

Early prehistoric people with practical knowledge but little science struggled for protection against natural disasters that they had no physical ability to prevent. In desperation they looked to the sun and moon – perhaps through them to the powers of their ancestors, whose spirits

40. Balquhain recumbent stone circle and outlier, Aberdeenshire.

11
Further reading

Brennan, M. *The Stars and the Stones.* Thames & Hudson, 1983.

Burl, A. *Megalithic Brittany: A Guide to Over 350 Sites and Monuments.* Thames & Hudson, 1985.

Burl, A. *The Stonehenge People.* Dent, 1987.

Burl, A. *From Carnac to Callanish: The Prehistoric Stone Rows and Avenues of Britain, Ireland and Brittany.* Yale University Press, 1993.

Burl, A. *The Stone Circles of Britain, Ireland and Brittany.* Yale University Press, 2000.

Castleden, R. *The Making of Stonehenge.* Routledge, 1993.

Castleden, R. *Britain 3000 BC.* Sutton, 2003.

Childe, G. *The Bronze Age.* Cambridge University Press, 1930.

Darvill, T. *Prehistoric Britain.* Batsford, 1987.

Fergusson, J. *Rude Stone Monuments in All Countries: Their Age and Uses.* John Murray, 1872.

Hawkins, G. S., with White, J. B. *Stonehenge Decoded.* Souvenir, 1966.

Heggie, D. C. *Megalithic Science.* Thames & Hudson, 1981.

Heggie, D. C. (editor). *Archaeoastronomy in the Old World.* Cambridge University Press, 1983.

Hoskin, M. *Tombs, Temples and Their Orientations.* Ocarina, 2001.

Jones, A. 'On the earth-colours of Neolithic death', *British Archaeology*, 22 (1997), 6.

Le Roux, C-T. *Gavrinis et les Iles du Morbihan.* Ministère de la Culture, Rennes, 1985.

Lockyer, Sir N. *Stonehenge and Other British Monuments Astronomically Considered.* Macmillan, second edition 1909.

Lynch, F. 'Colour in prehistoric architecture' in *Prehistoric Ritual and Religion*, edited by A. Gibson and D. Simpson. Sutton, 1998.

MacKie, E. W. *Science and Society in Prehistoric Britain.* Elek, 1977.

Ruggles, C. L. N. *Astronomy in Prehistoric Britain and Ireland.* Yale University Press, 1999.

Ruggles, C. L. N., and Burl, A. 'A new study of the Aberdeenshire recumbent stone circles. 2: Interpretation', *Archaeoastronomy*, 8, S25-60 (1985).

Ruggles, C. L. N., and Whittle, A. W. R. (editors). *Astronomy and Society in Britain during the Period 4000–1500 BC.* British Archaeological Reports, 88 (1981).

Shee Twohig, E. *The Megalithic Art of Western Europe.* Oxford University Press, 1981.

Smith, J. *Choir Gaur: The Grand Orrery of the Ancient Druids,*

Commonly Called Stonehenge. Salisbury, 1771.
Somerville, H. B. 'Instances of orientation in prehistoric monuments of the British Isles', *Archaeologia*, 73 (1923), 193–224.
Stukeley, W. *Stonehenge: A Temple Restor'd to the British Druids*. Innys & Manby, 1740.
Thom, A. *Megalithic Sites in Britain*. Oxford University Press, 1967.
Thom, A. *Megalithic Lunar Observatories*. Oxford University Press, 1971.
Thom, A., Thom A. S., and Burl, A. *Megalithic Rings: Plans and Data for 229 Monuments in Britain*. British Archaeological Reports, 81 (1980).
Thom, A., Thom, A. S., and Burl, A. *Stone Rows and Standing Stones, I, II*. British Archaeological Reports, International Series, 560 (1990).
Wood, J. E. *Sun, Moon and Standing Stones*. Oxford University Press, 1978.

Minor references for chapter 8

Boece, Hector. See: Allcroft, H. *The Circle and the Cross, I*. Macmillan, 1927.
Byron, Lord. *Don Juan*, Canto 11, 25, *c*.1820.
Defoe, D. *A Tour through the Island of Great Britain*. Yale University Press, 1991.
Engleheart, G. *Antiquity*, 4 (1930), 49.
Keiller, A. *Megalithic Monuments of North-East Scotland*. Vacher, 1934.
Logan, J. *Archaeologia*, 22 (1829), 201.
Peet, T. E. *Rough Stone Monuments and Their Builders*. Harper Brothers, 1912.

72

Index

Page numbers in italic refer to illustrations.